F-16
Worldwide Markings
By Lou Drendel

Color artwork by Lou Drendel, Don Greer and Dave Gebhardt

FA-71
60 TH ANNIVERSARY

BELGIAE GALLORUM FORTISSIMI

Squadron Signal Publications

350 FIGHTER SQUADRON

Cover: An F-16C aggressor of the 57th Fighter Weapons Wing about to bounce another F-16 during Red Flag exercises over the Nellis Range. (Painting by Lou Drendel)

Title Page: In July 2001, the vertical fin of Belgian Air Force F-16A-20 MLU (s/n FA-71) was painted to celebrate the sixtieth anniversary of that air arm's 350 Squadron. Three years earlier, FA-71 had carried what are arguably some of the most colorful markings ever displayed on a Fighting Falcon (see page 64). I nset: F-16A-20 MLU s/n 659 of the Royal Norwegian Air Force.

Back Cover: An F-16C of the Israeli Air Force "Scorpion Squadron." (Painting by Lou Drendel)

ISBN 0-89747-510-0

If you have any photographs of aircraft, armor, soldiers or ships of any nation, particularly wartime snapshots, why not share them with us and help make Squadron/Signal's books all the more interesting and complete in the future? Any photograph sent to us will be copied and the original returned. The donor will be fully credited for any photos used. Please send them to:

Squadron/Signal Publications, Inc.
1115 Crowley Drive
Carrollton, TX 75006

Если у вас есть фотографии самолетов, вооружения, солдат или кораблей любой страны, особенно, снимки времен войны, поделитесь с нами и помогите сделать новые книги издательства Эскадрон/Сигнал еще интереснее. Мы переснимем ваши фотографии и вернем оригиналы. Имена приславших снимки будут сопровождать все опубликованные фотографии. Пожалуйста, присылайте фотографии по адресу:

Squadron/Signal Publications, Inc.
1115 Crowley Drive
Carrollton, TX 75006

軍用機、装甲車両、兵士、軍艦などの写真を所持しておられる方はいらっしゃいませんか？どの国のものでも結構です。作戦中に撮影されたものが特に良いのです。Squadron/Signal社の出版する刊行物において、このような写真は内容を一層充実し、興味深くすることができます。当方にお送り頂いた写真は、複写の後お返しいたします。出版物中に写真を使用した場合は、必ず提供者のお名前を明記させて頂きます。お写真は下記にご送付ください。

Squadron/Signal Publications, Inc.
1115 Crowley Drive
Carrollton, TX 75006

Introduction

The F-16 Fighting Falcon, also known as the "Viper," has become the most popular modern fighter in the world. It is currently operated by twenty-four different countries. It has been over thirty years since the F-16 made its first flight from Edwards Air Force Base, and in those years, the F-16 has been reinvented time and time again through numerous upgrades.

The F-16 was originally conceived by purists John Boyd and Pierre Sprey, who recognized the need for a fighter to compete with the light and fast MiGs that were proving the efficacy of gun-fighting in the skies of Vietnam. They envisioned a daytime, visual flight rules (VFR) only, point defense interceptor and dogfighter relying on an internal cannon and short-range heat-seeking missiles. The Lightweight Fighter Competition of the early 1970s produced just such an airplane in the YF-16. But that is not the airplane that was eventually produced.

The F-16 has morphed into the most versatile multimission fighter ever built. The capabilities inherent in the basic airframe design have led to many additional, if slight, modifications to the basic shape of the Viper. The "lightweight fighter," foisted upon the defense establishment by the "Fighter Mafia" of Boyd, Sprey, and their associates within the Pentagon, has become the darling of the military as its mission continues to expand.

Armed with an internal cannon plus radar-guided and heat-seeking missiles, the F-16 remains a potent air superiority fighter. Equipped with laser and infrared targeting pods, it becomes a deadly accurate strategic and/or tactical bomber. It has performed all of these missions superbly.

Through all of the modifications, the basic F-16 camouflage has remained little changed, although some international F-16 customers have applied their own camouflage, based on local requirements. Almost all F-16 units everywhere have applied some form of unique markings.

F-16s have been at the forefront of recent conflicts, and we have devoted a chapter to the markings applied to aircraft and weapons in Operations Desert Storm and Iraqi Freedom.

Acknowledgements

This book would not have been possible without the support of F-16 photographers worldwide. Ted Carlson, Andre Jans, Cor van Gent, Stefaan Ellebaut, Neil Jones, Rene Wilthof, Emiel Bonte, Ofer Zidon, Chris Lofting, Yuval Lapid, Ian Nightingale, Roel Reijne, Koen Leuvering, Menso van Westrhenen, Marlene Leutgeb, Mark Wright, Kent Scott, and S.L. Tsai all helped with photos of foreign Vipers. Scott Brown sent many, many pictures taken by himself, Sean Hampton, and Mark Snodgras at Balad AB in Iraq. Lockheed Martin and the USAF were the source of many of the USAF photos. The technical details came from a variety of Internet sources, chief among them www.F-16.net and the very extensive files of Joe Baugher, two of the most in-depth sources of worldwide Viper information. All have my heartfelt gratitude.

▲ F-16A-10 (s/n 80-0524) of the 148th Fighter Squadron (FS), 162nd Fighter Group (FG), Arizona Air National Guard (ANG), 19 May 1995. This aircraft was retired to the Aerospace Maintenance and Regeneration Center (AMARC), Davis-Monthan AFB, Tucson, Arizona, 16 June 2000. (Ted Carlson, Fotodynamics)

▼ F-16C-30A (s/n 85-1458) of the 457th FS, 301st Fighter Wing (FW), NAS Fort Worth Joint Reserve Base, Fort Worth, Texas. The 301st is the only Air Force Reserve fighter unit in Texas. (Ted Carlson, Fotodynamics)

▼ F-16C-50C (s/n 91-0352), demonstration aircraft of the 52nd FW, Spangdahlem Air Base, Germany, 16 July 2005. (Stefaan Ellebaut)

▼ A pair of F-16 Fighting Falcons (F-16C-25 s/n 83-1137 and F-16C-25D s/n 84-1247) fly a sortie for the weapons systems evaluation program at Tyndall Air Force Base, Florida. The F-16s are assigned to the 194th FS, 144th FW, California ANG. (USAF photo by Master Sgt. Shaun Withers)

▲ An F-16C-30F (s/n 87-0236) flies in formation with a MiG-29 over Krezesiny Air Base, Poland, during exercise Sentry White Falcon 2005. The F-16 is assigned to the 170th FS, 183rd FW, Illinois ANG, in Springfield. (USAF photo by Tech. Sgt. Shaun Kerr)

▼ F-16C-50P (s/n 92-3921) assigned to the 522nd Fighter Squadron, (FS), 27th FW, Cannon AFB, New Mexico, heads out for a mission over the Nevada Test and Training Ranges during Red Flag 04-3 on 20 August 2006. More than a hundred aircraft and 2,500 participants are involved in Red Flag, a realistic combat training exercise involving the U.S. Air Force and its allies. (USAF photo by Tech. Sgt. Kevin Gruenwald)

▼ An F-16C of the 524th FS, 27th FW, on 5 April 1997. (Ted Carlson, Fotodynamics)

▲ A pair of F-16Cs of the 419th FW (AFRC) from Hill AFB, Utah, on 28 June 2001. (Ted Carlson, Fotodynamics)

▲ F-16C-40B (USAF s/n 88-0419) of the 388th FW, (ACC) Hill AFB, Utah, on 20 April 2000. (Ted Carlson, Fotodynamics)

▲ F-16C-40B "Buzzard 1" (USAF s/n 88-0413) of the 31st FW (USAFE), Aviano Air Base, Italy. (Ted Carlson, Fotodynamics)

▼ The F-16s of the "Jersey Devils" carry a devil's head on the fuselage. (Ted Carlson, Fotodynamics)

▲ F-16C-25B (s/n 83-1148) of the 119th FS, 177th FW, New Jersey ANG, Atlantic City International Airport, New Jersey, at March Air Reserve Base, California, 16 April 2003. (Ted Carlson, Fotodynamics)

▼ F-16C-50D (USAF s/n 91-0399) of the 13th FS takes off from Misawa Air Base, Japan, while participating in Exercise Keen Sword 2005. Keen Sword is a joint, bilateral defense exercise with U.S. Forces in Japan and the Japanese Self-Defense Forces. A "Wild Weasel" squadron, the 13th FS generates and flies interdiction, offensive and defensive counter-air, and suppression of enemy air defense sorties. During Operation Desert Strike, it was credited with HARM kills on an Iraqi SA-8 and ROLAND radar missile system. (USAF photo by Staff Sgt. Cherie A. Thurlby)

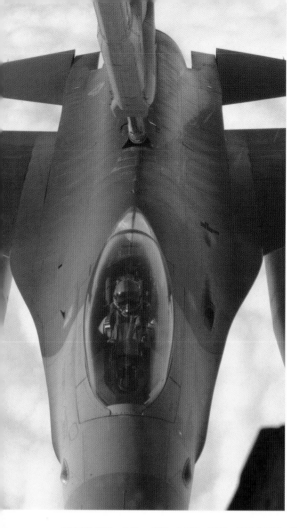

▲ An F-16C-30A (s/n 85-1448) of the 114th FW, South Dakota ANG, at Joe Foss Field Municipal Airport, Sioux Falls, South Dakota.

◄ An F-16 receives fuel from a KC-10A Extender of the 908th Expeditionary Aerial Refueling Squadron during a combat patrol over Iraq on Christmas Day 2005. (USAF photo by Senior Master Sgt. Mark Moss)

▶ F-16Cs of the 174th FW of the New York Air National Guard at Hancock Field, New York. Foreground aircraft is an F-16C-25 (s/n 83-1155). (Andre Jans)

▼ F-16C-30D of the 162nd FS, 178th FW (FTU), Ohio ANG, at Beckley-Springfield Municipal Airport, Ohio. This Viper flew forty missions in Operation Desert Shield. (Andre Jans)

▲ This F-16C is loaded for a SEAD (Suppression of Enemy Air Defenses) mission with AGM-88 High-speed Anti-Radiation Missiles (HARMs), AIM-9M Sidewinders, and AIM-120 Advanced Medium-Range Air-to-Air Missiles (AMRAAMs). (USAF photo)

▲ F-16 Fighting Falcons from the 62nd Fighter Squadron, Luke AFB, Arizona, over southern Florida during a flight from Luke to Key West, Florida, to fly training missions with Navy F-18 pilots. (USAF photo by Tech. Sgt. Jeffrey Allen)

▼ This F-16C-30F (s/n 87-0242) carries the flagship markings of the 86th Tactical Fighter Wing. It flew fifty-five missions in Operation Desert Storm with the 614th Tactical Fighter Squadron (TFS). (Andre Jans)

▲ Brig. Gen. Jeff Riemer climbs down from the cockpit of the last of 2,231 F-16s produced for the Air Force (s/n 01-7053), shortly after flying it from the Lockheed Martin plant in Fort Worth to Shaw AFB, South Carolina, on 18 March 2005. Riemer was the System Program Office director when the F-16 contract was awarded and is now the director of operations at Air Force Materiel Command headquarters. While Lockheed will continue to produce F-16s for international coalition partners, the USAF will receive no more. The first delivery was in 1978. (USAF photo by Staff Sgt. Josef E. Cole III)

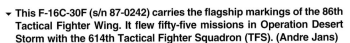

◄ Two F-16s (F-16C-42H s/n 90-0727, foreground; F-16C-32H s/n 87-8307, background) from the 64th Aggressor Squadron (AS) at Nellis AFB wait to be refueled by a KC-135 Stratotanker during a Red Flag mission. The F-16s of the 64th have a unique paint scheme to match their role as simulated enemy MiG aircraft during quarterly Red Flag exercises. Like the MiGs they simulate, both F-16s carry *"bort"* numbers. *"Bort"* is a Russian word, denoting the Bureau Number or construction number used to identify military aircraft. (USAF photo by Master Sgt. Robert W. Valenca)

▼ F-16C-42H s/n 90-0727 (*bort* 27) from Nellis AFB prepares to take off and fly as a team aggressor during William Tell 2004 at Tyndall AFB, Florida, 8 November 2004. The two-week William Tell competition challenges pilots, weapons loaders, and maintainers from five F-15 fighter wings. (USAF photo by Staff Sgt. Josef Cole)

◄ A pair of 64th AS F-16s bank over the Nellis AFB range. (USAF photo)

▲ F-16C-32D (s/n 86-0269) from Nellis AFB flies in its role as an aggressor during Exercise William Tell 2004. It carries red *bort* number 69 in its role as a simulated MiG-29. (USAF photo by Staff Sgt. Dennis J. Henry)

▲ F-16C-32J (s/n 87-0321, *bort* number 21) aggressor of the 414th CTS (Combat Training Squadron) over the Nevada Desert. Activated on 1 November 1991 as the 414th Composite Training Squadron to replace the then-inactive 64th and 65th Aggressor Squadrons, the 414th CTS used the F-16 to simulate various foreign air force fighters and tactics during periodic Red Flag exercises at Nellis AFB. The 64th Aggressor Squadron was reactivated on 3 October 2003, again flying the F-16. (Ted Carlson, Fotodynamics)

▸ F-16s from the 64th AS at Nellis AFB are lined up ready for action during William Tell 2004 at Tyndall AFB, Florida, 13 November 2004. This was the fiftieth anniversary of the William Tell competition, which tests an aircrew's ability to perform under combat conditions. Aircraft in foreground is F-16C-32D s/n 86-0272. (USAF photo by Tech. Sgt. Kevin Gruenwald)

▾ A pair of "Top Gun" F-16As (F-16A-15AM OCU s/n 90-0943, foreground; and F-16A-15AM OCU s/n 90-0944, background) of the Naval Strike and Air Warfare Center (NSAWC) lands at NAS Fallon, Nevada, 11 September 2001. Both Vipers were originally ordered by Pakistan in 1992 but were embargoed. (Ted Carlson, Fotodynamics)

▲ A pair of F-16Cs (F-16C-32F s/n 87-0267, *bort* 67, foreground; F-16C-32D s/n 86-0269, *bort* 69, background) of the 414th CTS. Aggressor F-16s are painted in various foreign camouflage schemes to enhance their mission. *Bort* 69 carries the unit marking "414 CTS" on its vertical fin. Barely visible under the unit marking are the words "RED FLAG" in smaller capital letters. (Ted Carlson, Fotodynamics)

▼ An F-16C-32F (s/n 87-0267) of the 64th Aggressor Squadron (Red Flag) over Nellis AFB. (Ted Carlson, Fotodynamics)

▲ Thunderbird solo pilots team up over Nellis AFB to perform their trademark calypso pass. (USAF photo by Tech. Sgt. Sean M. White)

▸ Thunderbirds line up in close trail behind a tanker. (Ted Carlson, Fotodynamics)

▲ Capt. Christopher Stricklin ejects from the Thunderbirds' number six aircraft less than a second before it impacts the ground at Mountain Home AFB, Idaho, 14 September 2003. (USAF photo by Staff Sgt. Bennie J. Davis III)

▾ Throughout the twenty-three years the team has used the F-16, the Thunderbirds' markings have remained consistent (USAF photo)

▲ A view of the Thunderbirds from the slot position during the famed diamond takeoff at Nellis AFB. The takeoff is made in the "finger-four" formation. The number four (slot) pilot will slide into position to form the diamond as soon as ground clearance allows. (USAF photo by Tech. Sgt. Sean M. White)

▾ The Thunderbirds aerial demonstration team performs a loop while in the famous Delta formation near Eielson AFB, Alaska. The Thunderbirds transitioned from the T-38 to the F-16A in 1983. They were the last USAF unit to operate the F-16A and converted to the F-16C in 1992. (USAF photo by Tech. Sgt. Sean M. White)

11

USAF F-16s in Combat

◄ The first combat deployment for USAF F-16s was Operation Desert Storm, which started on 17 January 1991. F-16s performed 25 percent of strike sorties (300 to 400 daily) throughout the war, totaling 13,500 sorties. F-16s participated in the first daylight raid of Operation Desert Storm on 19 January 1991, attacking targets in Baghdad. Two F-16s from the 614th Tactical Fighter Squadron (TFS) were lost and the pilots taken prisoner. (USAF photo)

▲ F-16Cs of the 388th TFW lined up at Al Minhad Air Base during Operation Desert Shield, the buildup that preceded Desert Storm. Aircraft that can be identified are (front to rear) F-16C-40C, s/n 88-0452; F-16C-40B, s/n 88-0419 or s/n 88-0436 (both are known to have carried the "388ᵀᴴ TFW" unit marking); F-16C-40B, s/n 88-0429; and F-16C-40B, s/n 88-0422. (USAF)

▼ An F-16C-25F (s/n 85-1405) of the 10th TFS, 50th TFW, loaded with Mk 84 2,000-pound bombs and an ALQ-131 ECM pod on centerline. In December 1990, the 10th TFS and the 10th Aircraft Maintenance Unit deployed to the Persian Gulf and remained in support of Operation Provide Comfort. (USAF)

▼ During Operation Desert Storm, 249 USAF F-16s flew over thirteen thousand sorties in strikes against Iraq, the most of any Coalition aircraft. Five were lost in combat. The vast majority of these missions were daylight VFR with "dumb" bombs. (USAF)

F-16A-10 s/n 79-0293 of the South Carolina ANG flew forty-six missions in Operation Desert Storm. Initial Desert Storm air campaign plans tasked F-16s in large strike packages against targets such as airfields, chemical weapons storage areas, Scud missile production facilities, Republican Guard locations, leadership targets, and military storage facilities, mostly during the daylight hours. (USAF)

Ground personnel prepare this F-16C-30F (s/n 87-0258) of the 401st TFW, armed with Mk 84 bombs and AIM-9 Sidewinders, for a combat mission. (USAF)

F-16C-25C (s/n 84-1215) of the 17th TFS, 363rd TFW, based at Al Dhafra Air Base, on a "Kill Box" mission. F-16s attacked Republican Guard positions with CBUs in advance of the liberation of Kuwait. (USAF)

An F-16C-25 of the 10th TFS, 50th TFW. (USAF)

A pilot from the 401st TFW describes his initial war experiences for fellow pilots and intelligence debriefers. This F-16C-30F (s/n 87-0221) of the 614th TFS flew fifty-four missions in Operation Desert Storm. It carried the marking "614 TFS" on the port side of the vertical fin underneath the Torrejon Air Base code "TJ." The 401st TFW and its constituent squadrons were disbanded in 1991. (USAF)

F-16 s/n 87-0221 carried the marking "614 AMU" on the starboard side of its vertical fin. The 401st deployed from Torrejon Air Base, Spain, to Doha, Qatar, and during the forty-two days of Operation Desert Storm flew 1,303 combat missions and delivered 3.2 million pounds of weapons. Two 401st pilots became prisoners of war when their aircraft were lost during the first daylight raid on Baghdad. (USAF)

Staff Sgt. Jeff Lease (left) from the 35th Maintenance Squadron at Misawa Air Base, Japan, and Senior Airman Ben Ramaekers, from the 18th Munitions Squadron at Kadena Air Base, Japan, unload AIM-9 Sidewinder missiles at Incirlik Air Base, Turkey, to complete a munitions package for an F-16 of the 555th FS. Aircraft in background is an F-16C-40D (s/n 88-0535) of the 555th FS. (USAF)

An F-16CJ pilot checks right before taxiing to the active runway. (USAF)

An armament technician checks an AIM-120 AMRAAM missile on an F-16CJ Fighting Falcon before takeoff. The AMRAAM weighs 340 pounds and uses an advanced solid-fuel rocket motor to achieve a speed of Mach 4 and a range in excess of thirty miles. In long-range engagements, the AMRAAM uses inertial guidance and receives updated target information via a data link from the launch aircraft. It transitions to a self-guiding terminal mode when the target is within range of its own monopulse radar set. (USAF)

F-16C-30E (s/n 86-0336) of the 186th FS, Montana ANG, carries both laser-guided bombs (LGB) and a JDAM (Joint Direct Attack Munition). LGBs are guided to their targets by the targeting pod (on the starboard side of the intake), while the JDAM receives its targeting information via GPS. JDAM is a tail cone and fin assembly, containing an inertial navigation system/global positioning system guidance kit, that converts existing unguided free-fall bombs into accurate, adverse-weather, "smart" munitions. (USAF)

F-16C-30J (s/n 87-0328) of the 188th FS, 150th FW, New Mexico ANG. In 1994, the 150th Tactical Fighter Group (TFG) traded in its A-7s for state-of-the-art F-16C-40 Night Falcons equipped with the LANTIRN low-altitude night attack system. They also received a number of F-16C-30s to support tactical training at Fort Bliss, as well as some F-16Ds for pilot training. The "Tacos" of the 188th FS operated from Balad Air Base, Iraq, during Operation Iraqi Freedom. (Sean Hampton)

F-16C-40C (s/n 88-0471), loaded with a GBU-31 JDAM for a mission from Balad Air Base, Iraq. The "flagship" of the 421st FS, 366th FW, Hill AFB, Utah, this F-16 reached 6,000 flight hours during a 2006 Operation Iraqi Freedom deployment. (Scott Brown)

An F-16CJ of the 55th Expeditionary Fighter Squadron (EFS), 27th FW, Shaw AFB, South Carolina, on an Operation Northern Watch mission out of Incirlik, Turkey, prior to Operation Iraqi Freedom. It is armed with AIM-120 and AIM-9 air-to-air missiles and AGM-88 HARMs. (USAF)

▲ Nose art on F-16s of the 150th FW at Balad Air Base during Operation Iraqi Freedom. (Sean Hampton)

▲ Maj. Kelly Connell from the 180th FW at Toledo, Ohio, shuts down his F-16's engine at Morón Air Base, Spain, while on a mission in support of Operation Iraqi Freedom. In the background is an F-16 from the Oklahoma ANG. (USAF photo by Master Sgt. John E. Lasky)

▼ Airman 1st Class Mabel Arreola, a weapons loader assigned to the 35th FW at Misawa Air Base, Japan, unloads an AGM-88 HARM from an F-16 Fighting Falcon after a training mission at Nellis AFB. The AGM-88 is the primary weapon used to neutralize enemy radar sites. (USAF photo by Tech. Sgt. Kevin J. Gruenwald)

▲ Tail markings of an F-16C-30D (s/n 86-0309) of the "Vigilantes" of Montana ANG's 186th TFS at Balad Air Base, Iraq. (Sean Hampton)

▼ Tail markings on F-16C-30J (s/n 87-0328) of the 188th FS, 150th FW, New Mexico ANG. (Sean Hampton)

▼ Tail markings of an F-16C of the 421st FS "Black Widows" at Balad. The 421st flew Operation Iraqi Freedom missions from November 2004 to January 2005. (Scott Brown)

▲ F-16C-30J (s/n 87-0328) of the 188th FS, 150th FW, New Mexico ANG, at Balad Air Base, Iraq, in 2004, loaded with a pair of Guided Bomb Unit-12 (GBU-12) laser-guided bombs. The GBU-12 consists of a 500-pound general-purpose warhead, a nose-mounted laser seeker, and fins for guidance. The target is illuminated with a laser designator; the bomb then guides to a spot of laser energy reflected from the target. (Sean Hampton)

▼ F-16s of the 188th often carried mission tallies below the cockpit. Other art was applied in the field by imaginative crew chiefs. This is F-16C-30H (s/n 87-0314). (Sean Hampton)

▼ F-16C-30F (s/n 87-0231) of the 120th FS, 410th Air Expeditionary Wing, which operated from Azraq Air Base, Jordan, at the beginning of Operation Iraqi Freedom. (Sean Hampton)

▼ A pair of F-16Cs (F-16C-30E s/n 86-0358, 120th FS, 140th FW, Colorado ANG, front; F-16C-30D s/n 86-0309, 186th FS, 120th FW, Montana ANG, rear) prepares to depart Azraq Air Base on a combat mission. As many as five different squadrons operated from Azraq during the early stages of Operation Iraqi Freedom. (Sean Hampton)

17

▲ '328 came to grief when the left brake malfunctioned during a landing at Balad after an aborted night close support mission. The broken brake caused the Viper to depart the runway. (Sean Hampton)

▲ An F-16 from Shaw AFB, South Carolina, takes off from Aviano AB, Italy, in support of Operation Allied Force. (USAF photo by Senior Airman Delia A. Castillo)

▲ Mission markings on Vipers at Balad included GBUs, JDAMs, and even a strafing marker. (Sean Hampton)

▲ Senior Airman Timothy Nelson loads a bomb onto an F-16 Fighting Falcon at a forward-deployed location somewhere in Southwest Asia. He is deployed from the Indiana ANG at Fort Wayne. (USAF photo by Tech. Sgt. Regina Baker)

▲ Airman 1st Class Jason Lemke (left) and Staff Sgt. Paul Kaehler secure a GBU-12 onto an F-16 during a load crew competition at Osan Air Base, South Korea. Folding fin mechanism of the GBU-12 is shown in detail. (USAF photo by Airman 1st Class Stacie Good)

◀ Senior Airman David Rogers of the 13th Aircraft Maintenance Unit inspects an F-16's AIM-9 Sidewinder during exercise Keen Sword 2005 at Misawa Air Base, Japan. The Sidewinder is a supersonic, heat-seeking, air-to-air missile with a high-explosive warhead and an active infrared guidance system. (USAF photo by Staff Sgt. Cherie A. Thurlby)

▲ An F-16C-50D (s/n 91-0406) of the 23rd FS, 52nd FW, returns to Aviano Air Base, Italy, from a mission against targets in Yugoslavia, 2 April 1999. Members of the 52nd FW, from Spangdahlem Air Base, Germany, were deployed to Aviano in support of NATO Operation Allied Force. (USAF photo)

▼ A weapons load crew from the 22nd EFS loads a GBU-31 bomb on an F-16CJ from Spangdahlem Air Base, Germany, before a mission on 24 March 2003. The F-16CJs are assigned to this forward-deployed air base in support of Operation Iraqi Freedom. (USAF photo by Staff Sgt. Derrick C. Goode)

▼ Weapons loader Senior Airman William Russell (left) and load crew chief Tech. Sgt. Mark Worley, both from the Alabama ANG, detach a GBU-38 from an F-16 at a forward-deployed location in Southwest Asia. The GBU-38/B is a 500-pound JDAM using the Mk 82 bomb body and is considered a lightweight compared to most of the other munitions loaded on F-16s. It was used for the first time in Iraq. (USAF photo by Capt. Mae-Li Allison)

▼ USAF technicians perform an engine change on an F-16C (s/n 91-0342) of the 22nd EFS, 52nd FW, at Aviano AB. (USAF Photo)

▼ Iraqi Air Force Maj. Salam Shalaam discusses the cockpit layout of an F-16 Fighting Falcon with Maj. Jose Pinedo of the 421st EFS at Balad Air Base, Iraq. (Air Force photo by Staff Sgt. Ryan Hansen)

▲ An F-16C-25F (s/n 85-1406) from the "Green Mountain Boys" of the 134th FS, 158th FW, Vermont ANG, assigned to the 332nd Air Expeditionary Wing at Balad Air Base, Iraq, maneuvers to the post-contact position after an aerial refueling mission over Southwest Asia. (USAF photo by Tech. Sgt. Scott Reed)

◄ After spending the night at Ali Base, Iraq, because of a weather diversion, F-16 pilot Maj. Darren Censullo does a pre-flight walk around his aircraft before takeoff, 18 October 2004. A reservist, the major flew with the 332nd EFS at Balad Air Base, Iraq. He was deployed from the 482nd FW at Homestead Air Reserve Base, Florida. F-16s provide air support to Operation Iraqi Freedom coalition ground forces. (USAF photo by Tech. Sgt. Paul Dean)

▼ Crew chiefs marshal F-16s toward parking spots at a forward-deployed location in Southwest Asia. Airmen and aircraft from Hill AFB, Utah, are currently deployed supporting Operation Iraqi Freedom. (USAF photo by Master Sgt. Terry L. Blevins)

European F-16s

Netherlands

Norway

Belgium

Denmark

Turkey

Greece

Portugal

Poland

Italy

▲ F-16A-15 (s/n J-017), Royal Netherlands Air Force. The Netherlands was one of the four initial NATO customers for the F-16. The initial Dutch order for F-16A/B aircraft was for 102 aircraft — eighty single-seat F-16As and twenty-two-seat F-16Bs — which were to be assembled by Fokker. This line first opened in April 1978 and was the second of the European F-16 final assembly lines to open. (SABCA in Belgium was the first.) The first Dutch-built F-16 made its first flight on 3 May 1979 with test pilot Henk Temmen at the controls. Initial delivery of the F-16A/B to the Royal Netherlands Air Force (Koninklijke Luchtmacht – KLu) was in June 1979. (Andre Jans)

◄ F-16 (s/n 298) of the Royal Norwegian Air Force. In 1970, Norway started looking for a replacement for its aging fleet of F-104 Starfighters. Likely candidates included the Mirage F.1, Saab 37 Viggen, and the winner of the lightweight fighter competition (the Northrop F-17 or the F-16). On 21 July 1975, Norway, Belgium, the Netherlands, and Denmark ordered the F-16 and formed a consortium to build it under license. Norway acquired sixty F-16As and twelve F-16Bs from the Netherlands' Fokker production line between January 1980 and June 1984. (Stefaan Ellebaut)

◄ F-16B (s/n FB-24) from the former 2 Smaldeel/Escadrille, Force Aerienne Belge/Belgische Luchtmacht (2 Squadron, Belgian Air Force) at Leeuwarden Air Base, Netherlands, 7 February 1996. The Belgian Air Force was one of the first four international customers for the F-16. Belgium ordered 160 F-16s in two batches, but heavy attrition and restructuring of the armed forces reduced the number to seventy-two operational aircraft, all upgraded to MLU standard. The remaining aircraft have been stored or sold (fourteen to Jordan, for example). (Andre Jans)

▼ The Royal Danish Air Force (Flyvevåbnet) bought seventy-seven F-16A/Bs in two batches and two attrition replacement orders. Of these, forty-eight aircraft and fourteen spares all have been upgraded to Mid-Life Upgrade (MLU) standard and will remain operational until 2015-2020, when they will be replaced by the F-35 Joint Strike Fighter. (Andre Jans)

▲ A Belgian F-16A on final approach. Belgium was one of two European nations responsible for the European production of F-16s. (The other was the Netherlands.) The primary Belgian contractor in the F-16 program was Sociétés Anonyme Belge de Constructions Aéronautiques (SABCA), which was responsible for the final assembly of Belgian and Danish F-16s. (Mark McEwan)

▲ Cockpit close-up of Belgian F-16A-15AE OCU (s/n FA-118. (Rene Wilthof)

▼ F-16A-20 MLU (s/n FA-94) of 31 "Tiger" Squadron, Belgian Air Force, in a high-G turn, which produces vapor trails from the wing leading edge extensions. (Stefaan Ellebaut)

▸ F-16AM FA-56 of the Belgian Air Force at Kleine Brogel, Belgium. Tail markings on the port side were different. (Stefaan Ellebaut)

▼ Tail art on FA-87 of 31 Squadron at Kleine Brogel, Belgium. This F-16 made its first flight in the commemorative markings on 14 June 2005. (Stefaan Ellebaut)

F-16A-20 MLU (s/n FA-57) of the Belgian Air Force with tail markings celebrating the Tactical Discussion and Procedures Update (TDPU) 2005 multiservice exercise. Due to post-Cold War restructuring, the Belgian Air Force ceased to exist as an independent entity, becoming the Belgian Armed Forces Air Component (COMOPSAIR). (Rene Wilthof)

Belgian F16A-20 MLU (s/n FA-60) at RAF Fairford, 24 June 1999. The special color scheme commemorates the fiftieth anniversary of NATO. (Cor van Gent)

F-16A-20 MLU (s/n FA-134) of 10 Wing, Belgian Air Force, marked to celebrate the sixtieth anniversary of Kleine-Brogel Air Base, Belgium. (Stefaan Ellebaut)

F-16A-20 MLU (s/n FA-56) of the BAF at Kleine-Brogel. Tail markings commemorate twenty-five years of F-16 service with 349 Squadron. Each side of the tail had a different scheme. (Stefaan Ellebaut)

F-16A-10 (s/n FA-27) of 349 Squadron, BAF, at Kleine Brogel, Belgium, 16 November 1999, carries inert 500-pound Snakeye bombs. This aircraft was scrapped for spare parts reclamation, but now is to be restored and preserved. (Cor van Gent)

▲ F-16A-20 MLU (s/n FA-94) at Kleine Brogel, Belgium, on 28 April 2005, with special Tiger Meet tail markings. With the introduction of the Mid-Life Upgrade, other weapon systems could also be used. In addition to the AIM-120 and AGM-65 weapons, the Belgian Air Force acquired a batch of GBU-10, GBU-12, and GBU-24 laser-guided bombs in 2000. To make optimal use of these weapons, the Belgian government bought eight AN/AAQ-14 Sharpshooter targeting pods. About fifty sets of night vision goggles were also acquired to make it easier for the pilots to execute operations at night. (Stefaan Ellebaut)

▼ Port side of vertical fin of Belgian F-16A (s/n FA-122) at Beja, 6 July 2002. (Cor van Gent)

▼ F-16A-20 MLU (s/n 671) of 338 Squadron, Luftforsvaret (Royal Norwegian Air Force – RNoAF) at Payerne, Switzerland. (Stefaan Ellebaut)

▼ F-16A-20 MLU (s/n FA-122) of 31 "Tigers" Squadron, BAF, at Kleine Brogel Air Base on 3 September 2002. All seventy-two F-16s of the Belgian Air Force are assigned to NATO, with thirty-six aircraft (two squadrons) allocated to the Rapid Reaction Forces. FA-122 was written off in a mid-air collision in December 2003. (Cor van Gent)

▲ The starboard side of Norwegian F-16A (s/n 671) of 338 Squadron. The Royal Norwegian Air Force acquired sixty F-16As and twelve F-16Bs from the Netherlands' Fokker production line between January 1980 and June 1984. (Stefaan Ellebaut)

▾ Dutch F-16A-20 MLU (s/n J-138) of 315 "Lion" Squadron at Twenthe Air Base, with markings celebrating the fiftieth anniversary of the squadron.

▲ Starboard side of fin of J-138. (Stefaan Ellebaut)

▸ Belgian F-16A-15M (s/n FA-82) with 1994 Tiger Meet tail markings. (Stefaan Ellebaut)

25

▲ F-16A-5 (s/n 282) of 332 Squadron, RNoAF, lands in typical Norwegian winter conditions. Norway's short and snowy runways, which are often located at dispersed sites, dictated that their F-16s be fitted with braking parachutes to handle situations where ordinary wheel brakes could not be used. These chutes are housed inside a large rectangular extension at the base of the tail fin. Norwegian F-16s were the first F-16s to be fitted with parachutes.

▼ F-16A-20 MLU (s/n FA-61) of 23 Squadron, Belgian Air Force, at Klein Brogel on 22 August 2001, in markings commemorating the fiftieth anniversary of the squadron, which has since been disbanded. All seventy F-16s of the Belgian Air Component are assigned to NATO, with thirty-six aircraft (two squadrons) allocated to the Rapid Reaction Forces. (Cor van Gent)

▼ F-16A (s/n FA-67) of the Belgian Air Force at Kleine-Brogel Air Base in September 1995. (Stefaan Ellebaut)

▼ F-16A-20 MLU of 23 "Devils" Squadron, Belgian Air Force, at Kleine Brogel Air Base. (Stefaan Ellebaut)

▲ Port side of Belgian F-16A-15AC (s/n FA-116) of 31 "Tiger" Squadron at Klein Brogel on 22 August 2001 in 2001 Tiger Meet markings. In 1979 Belgium decided to adopt the Loral RAPPORT III (Rapid Alert Programmed Power Management and Radar) internal electronic countermeasures suite. Part of the system is carried in an extended fairing at the base of the tail fin, offering the advantage of neither using a hardpoint nor adding to overall aircraft drag. (Cor van Gent)

▼ Starboard side of FA-116. Markings celebrate the fiftieth anniversary of 31 Squadron. Installation of CARAPACE, a passive electronics counter-measure system, allowed Belgian F-16s to be used in operations such as NATO peacekeeping missions over Bosnia. CARAPACE-modified F-16s can be easily recognized by the fairing under the intake and the radar warning receivers in the drag chute compartment. (Cor van Gent)

▼ Another view of Belgian F-16A (s/n FA-94) of 31 "Tiger" Squadron in Tiger Meet tail markings. (Stefaan Ellebaut)

27

▲ The BAF's FA-118 of 2 Squadron wore this special tail marking for the 2002 Recce Meet at Florennes.

▼ Belgian F-16A (s/n FA-72) in a special livery commemorating the eightieth birthday of 2 Squadron in 1997. (Cor van Gent)

▲ Tail markings on this Belgian F-16A-20 MLU (s/n FA-112), seen at at Florennes on 16 September 2003, commemorated the eighty-fifth anniversary of 1 Squadron "Stingers." (Cor van Gent)

◄ Vertical fin of FA-112. (Cor van Gent)

▼ An F-16A-20 MLU (s/n FA-93) of 31 Squadron, Belgian Air Force, at Twenthe. (Cor van Gent)

▲ F-16A-20 MLU (s/n J-063) at Leeuwarden Air Base, in markings commemorating the sixtieth anniversary of 322 "Polly Parrot" Squadron, KLu. On 24 March 1999, J-063, part of the Dutch-Belgian DATF based at Amendola AFB in Southern Italy, intercepted a Serbian MiG-29 on radar. Pilot Maj. Peter Tankink fired an AIM-120 missile, scoring the first Dutch kill since World War II. (Rene Wilthof)

▲ F-16B-20 MLU (s/n J-270) of 306 Squadron, KLu, at Volkel Air Base, 2003, in markings celebrating the fiftieth anniversary of the squadron. (Cor van Gent)

▲ F-16B-2 MLU (s/n J-657) of 313 Squadron, KLu, at Beja on 5 June 2002 in a special color scheme for the 2002 Tiger Meet. J-657 is now s/n 736, Grupo 8, Fuerza Aérea de Chile (FACh - Chilean Air Force).

▸ F-16A-20 MLU (s/n J-055) of the Royal Netherlands Air Force F-16 display team. Personnel from 306, 311, and 312 Squadrons, the F-16 squadrons based at Volkel, comprise the team, which consists of one display pilot, two coaches, and five specialists. The display pilot for the 2006 season was Capt. Gert-Jan "Goofy" Vooren. The paint scheme is unique. (Mark Wright)

▲ J-055 performs at Coxyde, Belgium. (Stefaan Ellebaut)

▼ J-055 lands after a performance. (Rene Wilthof)

▲ The Dutch demo F-16 releases flares to accentuate a maneuver during its routine. Smoke generators are contained in canisters attached to the wingtip missile launchers. (Rene Wilthof)

◄ KLu F-16B-5 (s/n J-265) in the fortieth anniversary markings of 313 Squadron, seen on final approach in 1993. In 2003 the Dutch government decided to cut the F-16 force by 25 percent. In 2004, the KLu began providing NATO with 108 F-16s, with ninety of these available for deployments. (Andre Jans)

▼ F-16s from four different Dutch Viper squadrons lined up for takeoff. On 21 November 2005, Jordan signed a letter of intent to buy three Dutch F-16s, all two-seaters with the mid-life upgrade (s/ns J-650, J-653, and J-654) to be delivered in 2006. In December 2005 the Chilean government signed a contract with the Netherlands to obtain up to eighteen Dutch F-16s (eleven A-models and seven B-models). These will form a new squadron in addition to newly delivered Block 50 F-16s. (Rene Wilthof)

▲ F-16A-20 MLU (s/n J-647) of the KLu. This aircraft was built as a Block 15 model and was delivered in 1983. (Rene Wilthof)

▼ F-16A-5 (s/n J-230) of 323 Squadron, KLu, at Volkel Air Base on 29 July 1999. This was one of the F-16s marked with Peter van Stigt's very attractive rendition of the squadron's namesake, Diana, Princess of the Hunt. (Cor van Gent)

◄ F-16A-20 MLU (s/n J-516) of 311 "Eagle" Squadron, KLu, undergoes maintenance at Volkel Air Base. Eagle Squadron is a dedicated reconnaissance unit. (Koen Levering)

▼ As a long-time user of the F-16, the KLu maintains a separate flight test unit, Kantoor Testvliegen (KTV), at Leeuwarden Air Base, where the unit uses this specially instrumented F-16B-20 MLU (s/n J-653) for testing purposes. Seen here on final approach, it carries flight test instrumentation on missile launch rails. (Rene Wilthof)

▲ F-16A-5 (s/n J-234) of 315 Squadron, KLu, Twenthe Air Base, 29 March 2004. Delivered in 1981, J-234 served three squadrons of the RNLAF during its career. It became an instructional airframe in 1998, and 315 Squadron has been disbanded as part of the Dutch drawdown of forces. (Cor van Gent)

▸ F-16A-5 s/n J-236 was painted in these special markings to celebrate the eighty-fifth anniversary of the KLu. It is seen here at Leeuwarden Air Base on 3 July 1998. (Cor van Gent)

▾ F-16A-20 MLU (s/n J-366) of 313 Squadron, KLu, at Twenthe Air Base on 29 March 2004. The special tail marking commemorates the fiftieth anniversary of 313 Squadron. (Cor van Gent)

▲ F-16A-10C (s/n J-257) of 315 Squadron, KLu, at Twenthe Air Base on 8 December 1999. Tail marking celebrates the forty-fifth birthday of the squadron. J-257 has since received the Block 20 Mid-Life Upgrade. (Cor van Gent)

▲ F-16B-15U (s/n J-210) of 314 Squadron "Redskins," KLu, at Gilze-Rijen Air Base, 1995. Tail markings commemorate the disbanding of 314 Squadron. J-210 received the Block 20 Mid-Life Upgrade and was assigned to 323 Squadron. (Andre Jans)

▲ Fiftieth anniversary markings on F-16A-1 (s/n J-215) of 322 "Polly Parrot" Squadron, KLu, 1993. This aircraft is now on static display at the RNLAF military museum at Soesterberg Air Force Base. (Andre Jans)

▶ F-16A-10A (s/n J-248) of 323 Squadron, KLu, Volkel Air Base, 29 July 1999. This Viper sported the final and most notable version of Peter van Stigt's Diana tail art, which celebrated the squadron's fiftieth anniversary. Fighter pilots loved it; the censors did not. (Cor van Gent)

▼ A more prosaic tail marking on this KLu F-16A-5 (s/n J-231) celebrated the fiftieth anniversary of NATO. (Andre Jans)

NATO 1949 - 1999 OTAN

J-231

▲ F-16A-20 MLU (s/n E-603) of the Royal Danish Air Force (Flyvevåbnet) on final approach. (Chris Lofting)

◄ F-16B-20 MLU (s/n ET-022) of the Flyvevåbnet. The Royal Danish Air Force bought seventy-seven F-16A/B aircraft in two major batches and two attrition replacement orders. Of these, forty-eight aircraft and fourteen spares, all upgraded to MLU standard, will remain operational until 2015-2020, when they will be replaced by the F-35 Joint Strike Fighter. (Neil Jones)

▼ The initial Flyvevåbnet order was for forty-six single-seat F-16As and twelve two-seat F-16Bs. Final assembly of these planes, all built to the initial Block 1 standards, was carried out at the SABCA plant in Belgium. Deliveries to the RDAF began on 28 January 1980, with the arrival of the first F-16B. As all European-built F-16s were assigned USAF serials for administrative purposes, RDAF F-16s carry the last three digits of their USAF serial numbers on the fuselage, prefixed by either "E" (F-16As) or "ET" (F-16Bs). (Rene Wilthof)

This F-16A-20 MLU (s/n 665) of 331 Skvadron, Luftforsvaret (Royal Norwegian Air Force – RNoAF), was the first European F-16 to accumulate 5,000 flight hours and carried special markings to celebrate this feat. (Chris Lofting)

F-16B-20 MLU (s/n ET-198) of the Flyvevåbnet at Kleine Brogel, Belgium. It carries a special color scheme to celebrate the wedding of Prince Frederik of Denmark and Elisabeth Donnaldson of Tasmania. Their official monogram decorates the tail of the Viper. (Stefaan Ellebaut)

F-16A-10 s/n E-199 was one of the fifty-eight Block 1 F-16A/Bs in the initial Flyvevåbnet order later upgraded to F-16A/B Block 10 standards by the RDAF's Aalborg workshop in the Pacer Loft I program. It carried a special color scheme for the 1998 air show season. (Cor van Gent)

F-16A-20 MLU in the markings of 331 Skvadron, Luftforsvaret, carrying AIM-120 missiles and a unique targeting pod. In 2002, the Norwegian government sent F-16s to Afghanistan in support of Operation Enduring Freedom. These aircraft were stationed at Manas AFB in Kyrgyzstan along with aircraft from the Netherlands and Denmark. Operations were flown from October 2002 to October 2003, although Norway decided to withdraw its F-16s early. (Stefaan Ellebaut)

▸ F-16B-15AD OCU (s/n 711), 332 Skvadron, Luftforsvaret, at RAF Fairford, 24 July 1999, with markings celebrating the fiftieth anniversary of NATO. Block 15 OCU (Operational Capability Upgrade) aircraft are powered by the more reliable F100-PW-220 turbofan and have structural strengthening and upgraded systems. (Cor van Gent)

▾ Norwegian F-16A-20 MLU (s/n 659), at Nancy, on 20 June 1998. Royal Norwegian Air Force F-16s are equipped with the Northrop Grumman AN/ALQ-162 internally mounted deception jammer. In April 1998, Norway decided to acquire the Shadowbox II upgrade for the AN/ALQ-162. This increased the capability of the baseline jammer to deny lock-on by pulse-Doppler (PD) and airborne intercept (AI) radar threats. (Cor van Gent)

▾ A pair of F-16C-50s (s/n's 93-0665 and 93-0658) of Türk Hava Kuvvetleri, the Turkish Air Force (TuAF). Under the Peace Onyx I program, Turkey received 132 F-16Cs and twenty-four F-16Ds. The first eight aircraft in the order were built at Lockheed-Martin's Fort Worth, Texas, plant, but the remaining 148 aircraft were assembled in Turkey. The first two F-16Cs (both Lockheed-built F-16C-30s, s/n's 86-0066 and 86-0067) were delivered as assembly kits in March 1987, and the first F-16D was handed over in a ceremony at Fort Worth in July 1987. Production of the Peace Onyx I order ended with F-16C-40 s/n 93-0014. (Lockheed Martin)

▲ Tail markings of Turkish F-16D-50 (s/n 93-0696), delivered in 1997. Turkey provided eighteen F-16s to the allied campaign against Serbia. Eleven were stationed at the NATO base at Aviano, Italy, the remainder in Turkey. All were equipped with laser-guided bombs using the LANTIRN night-vision system. (Andre Jans)

▶ A pair of Greek F-16s. Each Hellenic F-16 is assigned a USAF serial number for administrative purposes and carries the last three digits of it as its local serial number. (Lockheed Martin)

▾ One of the latest Turkish Air Force F-16D-50s (s/n 94-1562), delivered in 1997. (Cor van Gent)

◀ Turkish F-16D-30E (s/n 87-0002) on final approach. (Menso van Westrhenen)

▾ Turkish F-16D-40 s/n 89-0042 was delivered in 1994. (Koen Luevering)

▲ F-16D-52 (s/n 537) of the Greek Air Force. Under the Peace Xenia III Foreign Military Sales Program, Greece ordered fifty brand-new F-16 Block 52 fighters equipped with conformal fuel tanks in June 2000 and exercised an option on ten more in September 2001. The order comprised forty F-16Cs and twenty F-16Ds. All were produced in just thirty-one months from receipt of the order, the last two being delivered on 8 June 2004. Normally it takes up to thirty-six to forty-two months to produce this many F-16s. (Neil Jones)

▲ Under Peace Xenia IV, on 13 December 2005 the Greek government ordered thirty new Block 52 F-16s with an option on ten more. The first batch consists of twenty C-models and ten D-models, with deliveries due in 2009. Total contract value was estimated at $3.1 billion if all options were exercised, but on 15 March 2006 the Greek government announced that it turned down the option to buy the ten additional aircraft. The HAF operates three F-16 wings: 110 *Pterix* (110th Wing) at Larissa Air Base, 111 *Pterix* at Nea Ankhialos Air Base, and 115 *Pterix* at Souda Bay Air Base. (Koen Luevering)

▸ Tail markings on Portuguese F-16A-15AV OCU (s/n 15109) of Esquadra 201. Under Peace Atlantis I, the Força Aerea Portuguesa (Portuguese Air Force – FAP) signed a letter of acceptance in December 1990 for twenty F-16 Block 15 OCU aircraft (seventeen A-models and three B-models) with Pratt and Whitney engines, including initial logistic support. (Ted Carlson, Fotodynamics)

▲ FAP F-16A (s/n 15109) at Nellis AFB for Red Flag exercises in 2000. During operation Allied Force in 1999, the FAP deployed three F-16s to Aviano Air Base in Italy, where they joined U.S. F-16s. Because the aircraft were not yet updated to MLU standards, they mainly performed combat air patrol missions and escorted offensive aircraft over Yugoslavian territory. (Ted Carlson, Fotodynamics)

▲ FAP F-16A (s/n 15109) lands at Monte Real Air Base, where both Portuguese F-16 squadrons are based. Portuguese F-16s have the identification light on the port side of the nose, and feature large bulges on the tail fin root which house the actuators for the tail planes. The actuators were relocated to make room for the installation of HF equipment and antenna. The B-models lack the HF antenna and the large bulges. (Rene Wilthof)

▼ This FAP F-16B (s/n 15118), seen at its base of Monte Real on 12 March 1998, was one of the initial three FAP B-models. Under Peace Atlantis II, in 1996 the FAP requested twenty-five re-engined USAF surplus F-16A/Bs, along with five spare F100-PW-220E engines. The surplus Block 15 aircraft were to be used in the ground attack role, replacing the FAP's fifty A-7Ps, beginning in 1998. (Cor van Gent)

◀ USAF Tech. Sgt. Brenton Baker (right), a life support technician with the Illinois ANG's 183rd FW, reviews F-16 ejection seat procedures with Polish Air Force Capt. Arkadiesz Kurkiewicz at Poznan, Poland, during the U.S. European Command exercise Sentry White Falcon in 2005. In 2006, the Polish Air Force began replacing its Soviet-made MiG fighters with F-16s as the country modernizes its military to NATO standards. Poland ordered forty-eight F-16C/D Block 52 aircraft, thus becoming the first former Warsaw Pact member to operate the F-16 Fighting Falcon. (USAF photo by Master Sgt. John E. Lasky)

▼ F-16B-5 (s/n MM7266), 18 Gruppo, Aeronautica Militare Italiana (Italian Air Force – AMI). Under program Peace Caesar, on 15 March 2001, the Italian government signed a letter of agreement for a five-year lease (with an option on another five years) of thirty-four F-16s and spares, in a deal worth up to $777 million over a ten-year period, as a stop-gap solution until delivery of the Eurofighter Typhoon.

▼ The F-16s provided to Italy have a standard ADF (air defense fighter) configuration. All aircraft received the uprated Pratt & Whitney F100-220E engine and underwent the Falcon-Up structural enhancement program. A number of weapon systems were released to the Aeronautica Militare Italiana (AMI) to be used in conjunction with the F-16s, including the AIM-120 AMRAAM missile. Italian F-16s are based at Cervia Air Base (5 Stormo, "Giuseppe Cenni") and Trapani-Birgi Air Base (37 Stormo, "Cesare Toschi").

Middle Eastern F-16s

Israel

United Arab
Emirates

Jordan

Bahrain

Egypt

Oman

▲ The first two of Israel's F-16Is (s/n's 407 and 408) landed at the Ramon Israel Air Force base in the Negev on 19 February 2004. The F-16I *Sufa* (Storm), a two-seater, is the latest version of the Lockheed Martin F-16. It is specially designed for Israel and is based on current Block 50/52 production aircraft. (Yuval Lapid)

▼ One of the original Peace Marble I F-16A-5s (s/n 107), of 116 "Flying Wing" squadron, is seen here landing at its home, Nevatim Air Base, Israel, 2 February 2005. The highest-scoring F-16 in the IDF/AF, it carries 6.5 kill markings, all from the 1982 Lebanon war, and the Operation Opera (Osirak nuclear reactor raid) participation emblem in addition to its squadron markings. The first F-16 deliveries to Israel (seventy-five Block 10 aircraft, except for eighteen F-16As and eight F-16Bs originally built as Block 5 but converted to Block 10) took place under the Peace Marble I Foreign Military Sales program. These planes were originally intended for the Imperial Iranian Air Force (IIAF), but the fall of the Shah in 1979 and the consequent rise of the Islamic fundamentalist regime caused these planes to be diverted to Israel. They had a number of internal changes that were unique to Israeli requirements, including the fitting of chaff/flare dispensers. The first four F-16s, known as *Netz* (Hawk) in *Tsvah Haganah Cheil Ha'avir* – Israel Defense Force/Air Force (IDF/AF) service arrived in Israel in July 1980 after an eleven-hour delivery flight. IOC was achieved a few weeks later. Combat debut of the F-16 was on 28 April 1981, when an IDF/AF F-16 of the "First Jet" Squadron shot down a Syrian Mi-8 helicopter over Riak, near the Lebanese town of Zahle. Five hours later, another Syrian Mi-8 fell prey to another F-16 of the same squadron. Of sixty-seven kills achieved by the F-16 worldwide, forty-seven are accredited to the IDF/AF's F-16s. (Ofer Zidon)

▲ F-16A-10 *Netz* (s/n 233) from 115 Squadron, the "Flying Dragon" squadron, which is based at Ovda Air Base and is used as the IDF/AF aggressor force. (Ofer Zidon)

▼ F-16D-40H *Barak* of 101 "First Fighter" Squadron at Tel Aviv (Jaffa)-Ben Gurion (Lod) (TLV / LLBG) Israel, 7 June 2005. While the F-16B is a two-seat version of the F-16A used for pilot conversion, the back seat of the Israeli F-16D *Barak* is occupied by a Weapons System Operator. Externally, this fighter differs from other F-16Ds by having a box-like extension, referred to as a dorsal spine, from the cockpit to the vertical stabilizer. (Ofer Zidon)

▲ IDF/AF F-16C-30 (s/n 359) of 110 "Knights of the North" Squadron landing at Ramat David Air Base, Israel, 2 February 2004. The Knights of the North Squadron was formed in 1953 and has flown Mosquitos, Vautours, Skyhawks, and Fighting Falcons in its long history. It has operated the F-16 since 1980 and was one of two squadrons that bombed the Iraqi nuclear reactor at Osirak in 1981. (Ofer Zidon)

▲ F-16A-10C, 116 Squadron, IDF/AF, at Ramon Israel, 19 February 2004. The last twenty-two of these aircraft were put on hold by the Reagan administration following Israel's raid on Iraq's Osirak nuclear reactor, and final deliveries did not take place until 1981. (Yuval Lapid)

▲ IDF/AF F-16I (s/n 408) makes its first local flight at Ramon, Israel, 20 February 2004. The F-16I is a multiple-role version of the F-16 conforming specifically to Israeli requirements. It is built to Block 52 standards, with a Northrop AN/APG-68(V)X fire-control radar, and is compatible with the LANTIRN system. The F-16I is known in IDF/AF service as the *Suefa* (Storm). (Ofer Zidon)

▲ Vertical fin of F-16A-10A (s/n 243) of 109 "Valley" Squadron, IDF/AF, seen here at Brno, Czech Republic, 4 April 2004. A chaff/flare dispenser on the tail is a standard feature of IDF/AF F-16s. This aircraft was one of an order originally intended for the Imperial Iranian Air Force, and was the eighth and final aircraft to bomb Iraq's Osirak nuclear reactor in Operation Opera. (Stefaan Ellebaut)

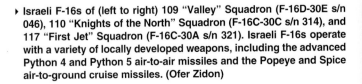

▲ Tail of F-16B-5 *Netz* (s/n 017) from the "Flying Wing" Squadron. This is another early F-16 from the IIAF order, lacking the chaff/flare dispensers on the tail. (Stefaan Ellebaut)

▸ Israeli F-16s of (left to right) 109 "Valley" Squadron (F-16D-30E s/n 046), 110 "Knights of the North" Squadron (F-16C-30C s/n 314), and 117 "First Jet" Squadron (F-16C-30A s/n 321). Israeli F-16s operate with a variety of locally developed weapons, including the advanced Python 4 and Python 5 air-to-air missiles and the Popeye and Spice air-to-ground cruise missiles. (Ofer Zidon)

43

▲ F-16B-5 *Netz* (s/n 989) of "Phoenix" Squadron carrying inert laser-guided bombs and Sidewinders. Prior to the establishment of the Phoenix Squadron Operational Training Unit in 2004, all IDF/AF weapon systems officers were trained on the job. (Chris Lofting)

▼ F-16D-40L (s/n 684) and F-16D-40K (s/n 648) *Baraks* from 105 "Scorpion" Squadron, IDF/AF, prepare to take off on a practice night sortie from Hatzor Air Base, May 2005. The Scorpion Squadron was activated with Block 40 *Baraks* in 1991. The new tail art and double spearhead on the drag chute housing were designed by Ra'anan Weiss. (Ofer Zidon)

▼ F-16C-40L *Barak* from 101 "First Fighter" Squadron, IDF/AF, October 2005. A portion of the original rudder markings remains under new tail art. (Ofer Zidon)

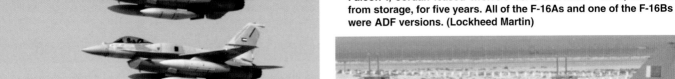

▲ F-16A-15C ADF (s/n 229) of 2 Squadron, Royal Jordanian Air Force (*Al Quwwat al Jawwiya al Malakiya al Urduniya*). Under Peace Falcon I, Jordan leased twelve F-16As and four F-16Bs, all taken from storage, for five years. All of the F-16As and one of the F-16Bs were ADF versions. (Lockheed Martin)

▲ An echelon of five F-16E/Fs from *Al Imarat al Arabiyah al Muttahidah*, (United Arab Emirates Air Force – UAEAF) shortly after arrival in the UAE. The UAE was the first customer for this advanced version of the F-16, and took delivery of a first batch of F-16E/F Block 60 aircraft in 2004. In 2005, the Gulf federation began upgrading two air force bases to support the new fighters. UAE pilots and personnel are trained at Tucson, Arizona. A number of Block 60 aircraft are based at Holloman AFB, New Mexico, for further testing. (Lockheed Martin)

▲ F-16-40CD (s/n 101) of 1 FS, Royal Bahrani Air Force. In March 1987, the government of Bahrain signed a letter of agreement for twelve F-16C/D Block 40 fighter aircraft (eight C's and four D's) under the Peace Crown Foreign Military Sales program. The first aircraft were accepted in March 1990 and arrived in Bahrain in May 1990. They were assigned to a single squadron based at Sheikh Isa Air Base on the east coast of the island.

▼ F-16-40Qs (s/n's 9951 and 9952) of the 252 Tactical Fighter Brigade, *Al Quwwat al Jawwiya Ilmisriya* (Egyptian Air Force – EAF). On 25 June 1980, Egypt signed a letter of agreement to acquire forty-two Block 15 F-16A/B fighters (thirty-four A-model single-seaters and eight B-model two-seaters) under the Peace Vector FMS program. (Lockheed Martin)

▲ F-16D-50 (s/n 801), 18 Squadron, *Al Quwwat al Jawwiya al Sultanat Oman* (Royal Air Force of Oman – RAFO). The aircraft delivered to Oman are equipped with General Electric F110-GE-129 engines and AN/APG-68(V)XM radars. Also included are fourteen Sniper advanced targeting pods with terrain-following radar. (Lockheed Martin)

◀ A formation of UAE F-16E/Fs. The Block 60 F-16, also known as the "Desert Falcon" (and F-16E/F in some circles), is the most advanced F-16 ever produced. An internal, forward-looking infrared navigation sensor mounted as a ball turret on the upper left nose distinguishes the Block 60 F-16 from previous versions. Other external characteristics include a targeting pod with faceted windows, no pitot tube, strip lighting on the wings and vertical tail, an air scoop on the forward right tail root, a small exhaust on the forward left tail root, and two other exhaust ports, one on either side of the lower rear portion of the engine inlet. Both single- and two-seat aircraft carry the conformal fuel tanks. (Lockheed Martin)

▼ F-16A, Royal Jordanian Air Force. The RJAF has two F-16 squadrons, 2 Squadron and 6 Squadron, both based at Al-Azraq Air Base.

▲ The first two Peace Vector I F-16A-15s for Egypt (s/n 9301 and s/n 9302) over the Giza pyramids. The first F-16 was accepted by *Al Quwwat al Jawwiya Ilmisriya* (the Egyptian Air Force) during a ceremony at Fort Worth in January 1982, with the first six planes arriving in Egypt on 16 March of that year. (Lockheed Martin)

▼ F-16F-60 (s/n 3012), 148 FS, UAEAF. The UAE purchased $2 billion in sophisticated aircraft armament for its F-16s, including 491 AIM-120B AMRAAM missiles, 267 AIM-9M Sidewinders, 163 AGM-88 HARMs, 1,163 AGM-65D/G Mavericks, fifty-two AGM-84 Harpoons, laser guided bombs, 20 mm ammunition, and other weaponry. (Sven De Bevere)

▾ F-16A-15R, s/n FA-94 (USAF s/n 80-3585), 31 "Tiger" Squadron, Belgian Air Force, 1991. The spectacular color scheme celebrated the fortieth birthday of the squadron.

▾ F-16C-32J, s/n 87-0321; 64th Aggressor Squadron, Nellis AFB, Nevada, 1989.

▾ F-16A-20 MLU, s/n 660 (USAF s/n 80-0660), 331 Squadron, Royal Norwegian Air Force, as seen at Twenthe Air Base, Belgium. Special markings commemorate twenty years of F-16 service with 331 Squadron and the squadron's sixtieth anniversary.

48

▾ F-16B-20 MLU, s/n FB-24 (USAF s/n 89-0012), F-16 Operational Conversion Unit, 10 Wing, Belgian Air Force, Kleine Brogel Air Base, Belgium. The special tail marking commemorates the fifteenth anniversary of the OCU.

▾ F-16A-20 MLU, s/n FA-122 (USAF s/n 88-0047), 31 Squadron, Belgian Air Force, April 2002. The tail painting was a special scheme for the 2002 Tiger Meet. This aircraft was destroyed in a crash following a mid-air collision with another F-16 on 9 December 2003.

▾ F-16C-52D "Wanna Play" (s/n 91-0370) of the 389th FS deployed with the 157th FS. It wore ten mission markings for Operation Enduring Freedom.

▲ F-16A-15AZ OCU, 403 Squadron, *KongTup Arkard Thai* (Royal Thai Air Force – RTAF). Under the Peace Naresuan Foreign Military Sales program, Thailand purchased eight F100-PW-220-powered Block 15 F-16As and four F-16Bs. Options for another six F-16As were exercised in mid-1987. Thailand took delivery of its first F-16A in a ceremony at Fort Worth in May 1988. The first batch of F-16s was assigned to 103 Squadron at Korat Air Base. Thai F-16s have the Westinghouse APG-66S fire-control radar, but they do have several nonstandard features, such as the ability to carry the Rafael Python 3 AAM. In addition, they can carry the Thomson-TRT Defense ATLIS-III automatic TV-tracking laser designator/range-finding pod. Six Rubis low-altitude night/bad-weather navigation pods were ordered from Thomson-TRT in November 1993. Sixteen more Block 15 OCU F-16A/Bs (twelve A's and four B's) were ordered in July 1992 under Peace Naresuan II. The first example of these was handed over in a ceremony at Fort Worth on 10 September 1995. These aircraft re-equipped No. 403 Squadron based at Takhli, which previously operated the F-5E/F. (RTAF)

Asian F-16s

Thailand

Republic of China (Taiwan)

Singapore

Indonesia

▲ Two F-16A-20 (s/n 93-0711, front, and s/n 93-0721, rear) aircraft on a training mission over the Arizona desert, seen from the backseat of an F-16B-20. Although carrying USAF markings, these aircraft are property of *Chung-kuo Kung Chun*, the Republic of China Air Force (RoCAF), and are operated on behalf of the Republic of China by the 21st FS "Gamblers" at Luke AFB, where they are used to train RoCAF pilots. (RoCAF photo)

▼ F-16B-20 (s/n 6821), 5 TFW, RoCAF. In November 1992, representatives of the Republic of China (Taiwan) and the United States signed an agreement for the sale of 150 F-16A/B aircraft (120 A-models and thirty B-models) to Taiwan under the Peace Fenghuang Foreign Military Sales program. (S.L. Tsai)

▲ F-16D-52J (s/n 94283) of the Republic of Singapore Air Force (RSAF). Singapore took delivery of its first Pratt & Whitney F100-PW-220 powered F-16 (a two-seater) on 20 February 1988. Although all aircraft are Block 15 models, they actually have strengthened Block 30 airframes. The aircraft were initially delivered to Luke AFB, where the RSAF trains its F-16 pilots. Singapore also leased nine F-16As previously used by the Thunderbirds flight demonstration team from 1993 to 1996, for training at Luke AFB. The first F-16s were not transferred to Singapore until January 1990. (Ian Nightingale)

▲ F-16B of the Royal Thai Air Force. (RTAF).

▲ The RoCAF F-16s are F-16-15 OCUs built to MLU specifications (but designated F-16-20). (RoCAF photo)

▼ F-16B-20 s/n 6830 was the last F-16B delivered to the RoCAF. The Block 20 models have the improved Westinghouse AN/APG-66(V)3 fire-control radar, AN/APX-111 IFF, ALR-56M advanced radar warning receivers, and the AN/ALE-47 chaff/flare dispensers. (S.L. Tsai)

▲ F-16C-52J (s/n 610) of the RSAF. The F-16C/Ds ordered by Singapore were all Block 52 aircraft and were powered by the Pratt & Whitney F100-PW-229 engine. The aircraft are provided with the Lockheed Martin "Sharpshooter," a downrated version of the LANTIRN pod system. All of the Singapore F-16C/Ds are equipped with wide-angle HUD and APG-68(V)5 radar and the Advanced Identification Friend or Foe (AIFF) system, which can be distinguished by an antenna array immediately forward of the cockpit. Interestingly, some of the F-16Ds in this order were equipped with a "swollen spine," similar to that of the Israeli F-16Ds, providing additional avionics capacity for air-to-ground missions. Delivery of these planes began in the spring of 1998. They are now serving alongside the F-16A/Bs at Tengah. (Menso van Westrhenen)

▲ Singapore placed a new contract in October 1997 for twelve Block 52D F-16C/Ds (six C's and six D's), purchased directly from the manufacturer and not through the U.S. Foreign Military Sales program. The first was delivered on 30 November 1999. The six F-16Cs replaced leased USAF F-16Cs used for training with the 425th FS at Luke AFB. The six Block 52D F-16Ds are operated by the 428th FS, 27th FW, at Cannon AFB, New Mexico. (Emiel Bonte)

▲ F-16-52J (s/n 611) of 140 Squadron, RSAF. Part of the deal for sale of additional F-16s to Singapore included a commercial lease-to-buy contract with Lockheed Martin for twelve Block 42 F-16C/Ds. These planes were leased for two and one-half years and remained in the United States, replacing nine leased USAF F-16A/Bs operating at Luke AFB. They are believed to have been purchased by the RSAF at the expiration of the lease. (Emiel Bonte)

▼ F-16D-52 (s/n 640) of 143 "Phoenix" Squadron (front) and F-16C-52 of 140 "Osprey" Squadron (rear), RSAF. Singapore squadrons include 140 Squadron at Tengah Air Base, 143 Squadron at Tengah Air Base, and 145 "Hornet" Squadron at Changi Air Base. F-16C/Ds are flown by 140 and 143 Squadrons, while 145 Squadron flies the D exclusively. The ten F-16D Block 52 aircraft ordered in 1994 have the same dorsal fairing as the Israeli F-16Ds and the sole VISTA aircraft, which is rumored to house an SPS-3000 self-protection jammer. The dorsal fairings were installed during assembly while the aircraft were on the production line in Fort Worth. (Menso van Westrhenen)

A pair of RoCAF F-16A-20s (s/n's 6685 and 6657) on takeoff from Hualien AFB, Taiwan, 23 October 2005. (S.L. Tsai)

F-16A-20 (s/n 6626) of the 21st TFG, RoCAF, at Chiayi AFB, Taiwan, 8 October 2005. The RoCAF operates nine squadrons of F-16s, including training squadrons in the United States. (S.L. Tsai)

F-16A-20 (s/n 6629) of the 22nd FS, RoCAF, on final approach. RoCAF F-16s are equipped with AIM-7M Sparrow, AIM-9M and AIM-P4 Sidewinder, and AGM-65 Maverick missiles. Recently a batch of 120 AIM-120C and fifty-four AGM-84 Harpoon missiles were purchased from the United States to complement the existing weapons stock. (S.L. Tsai)

▲ F-16B-20-CF of the 5th TFG, RoCAF, at Hualien AFB, Taiwan, 23 October 2005. (S.L. Tsai)

▲ The Tentara Nasional Indonesia-Angkatan Udara (Indonesian Air Force) received its first F-16 in December 1989, under the Peace Bima-Sena Foreign Military Sales program. Deliveries (eight F-16As and four F-16Bs) were completed in 1990. Serial numbers occupy the TS-1601/TS-1612 range. Painted in a smart blue/white/tan color scheme, the aircraft wear the national roundel on the left wing and have a parachute housing in the tail fairing. (Lockheed Martin)

▼ Indonesia only has one F-16 squadron, Skadron Udara 3, based at Iswahyudi Air Base. Aircraft in foreground is F-16B-15 s/n TS-1602.

▲ Indonesian F-16As on the ramp (s/n TS-1611 second in the line-up, with nose of F-16B-15 s/n TS-1602 in foreground). Indonesia equips its F-16s with only basic weaponry, including dumb bombs, AIM-9 missiles, and SUU-20 practice dispensers. Although capable of carrying out medium profile missions with its aircraft, the TNI-AU lacks funding to upgrade its F-16s and has left them configured as pure daytime dogfighters with a limited daytime attack capability. (Lockheed Martin)

▼ In November 1995, Indonesia expressed a need for sixty-four more F-16s, enough to equip four fighter squadrons, and expressed an interest in the twenty-eight embargoed Pakistani F-16s held in storage at AMARC. A contract was signed in 1996 for nine Block 20 F-16s. However, negotiations between the United States and Indonesia for the purchase of these planes were postponed in June 1997 because of Congressional objections to Indonesia's human rights record following riots in June 1996.

▲ "Cold Steel," F-16C-30A (s/n 85-1448) of the 175th FS, date unknown.

▲ "Miss Deal," F-16C-30A (s/n 85-1469) of the 175th FS, April 1992.

▲ "Satan, " F-16C-30A (s/n 85-1466) of the 175th FS, October 2002.

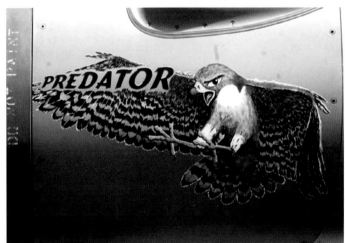

▲ "The Terminator," F-16C-30A (s/n 85-1472), 175th FS, date unknown.

▼ "Thumper," F-16C-30 (s/n 85-1440), 175th FS, April 1992.

▼ "Predator," F-16C-30A (s/n 85-1470), 175th FS, date unknown.

▼ "Speedy," F-16C-30A (s/n 85-1442), 175th FS, May 2001.

▼ "The King Lives," F-16C-30A (s/n 85-1454), 175th FS, date unknown.

▼ F-16A-20 MLU, s/n FA-106 (USAF s/n 87-0050), 349 Squadron, Belgian Air Force, Beauvechain, 2002. The tail marking celebrates the sixtieth anniversary of 349 Squadron (the "Blue Maces"). The dual-language Force Aerienne Belge/Belgische Luchtmacht was the first European nation to receive locally built F-16s, and 349 Squadron was the first F-16 squadron to be assigned to NATO.

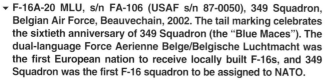

▼ NF-16D "VISTA" (variable-stability in-flight simulator test aircraft), s/n 86-048, USAF Test Pilots School, Edwards AFB, California. The VISTA F-16 is a highly modified F-16D used as a Vehicle Management System (VMS) and a test-bed for flight control systems. It also assists the Auto ACAS (Automatic Air Collision Avoidance System) project. The VISTA aircraft is a joint development of the U.S. Air Force Research Laboratory, Veridian Engineering Flight Research Group, and Lockheed-Martin Aeronautics, and is managed by the USAF Test Pilots School.

Emblem of the U.S. Air Force Test Pilots School.

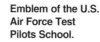

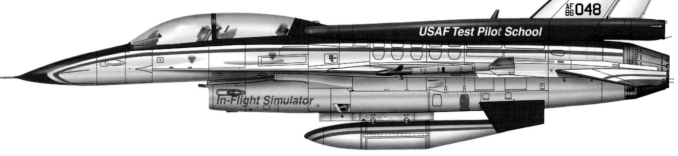

▼ F-16A-20 MLU, s/n FA-93 (USAF s/n 80-3584), 31 "Tiger" Squadron, Belgian Air Force, Kleine Brogel, Belgium. Tail markings are for the 2003 Tiger Meet. Tiger Meets began in 1959, when the Association of Tiger Squadrons was established to improve relationships between individual squadrons within NATO, and have been held annually since.

F-16C-30, s/n 87-0255, 182nd Fighter Squadron ("Lone Star Gunfighters"), 149th Fighter Wing, Texas Air National Guard, Kelly AFB, San Antonio, Texas, April 1999.

F-16C-42, s/n 89-2138, 125th Fighter Squadron ("Tulsa Vipers"), 138th Fighter Wing, Oklahoma Air National Guard, Tulsa International Airport, Tulsa, Oklahoma, June 2002. The 125th converted to the F-16C/D from the A-7D/K in 1993. Early squadron markings were a simple "Tulsa" in small white letters on the top of the fin and an "OK" tail code, but the Tulsa Vipers' F-16s now have one of the most colorful unit markings in the ANG.

F-16A-20 MLU, s/n FA-112 (USAF s/n 87-0056), of 1 Squadron ("Stingers"), 2 Wing, Belgian Air Force, 2003. Tail marking commemorated the 2003 Recce Meet held at Florennes Air Base, Belgium, and was carried only on the starboard side of the vertical fin. This aircraft was destroyed in a crash into the North Sea on 9 September 2005. The pilot, Cdt. Fabrice Massaux, was killed.

▾ F-16A-15AC OCU, s/n FA-111 (USAF s/n 87-0055), 1 Squadron, Belgian Air Force, Florennes, Belgium, 1997. The special color scheme honors the seventy-fifth birthday of the squadron. FA-111 subsequently received the Block 20 Mid-Life Upgrade.

▾ F-16C-30B (s/n 85-1552) of the 23rd Tactical Squadron, 52nd Tactical Fighter Wing, USAF Europe, Spangdahlem Air Base, Germany, 1991.

▾ F-16B-20, s/n 6830 (USAF s/n 93-0851), 5th Tactical Fighter Wing, Republic of China Air Force, Hualien, Taiwan.

Emblem of the 5th Tactical Fighter Wing, Republic of China Air Force.

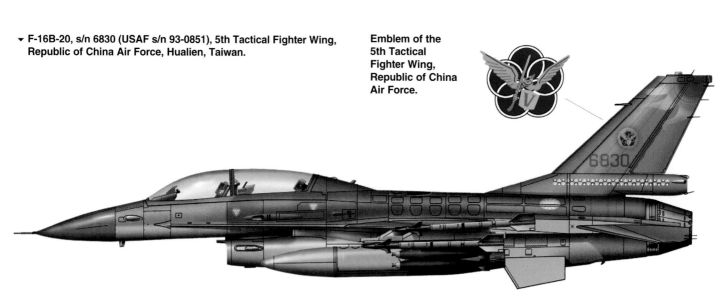

▾ **F-16B-20, s/n 6806 (USAF s/n 93-0827), 21st Tactical Fighter Squadron, 455th Tactical Fighter Wing, Republic of China Air Force, Chiayi Air Base, Taiwan, 2004.** While designated as Block 20 airplanes, RoCAF F-16s are actually F-16 Block 15 OCUs built to Mid-Life Upgrade specifications. The 21st FTS was the first RoCAF F-16 squadron.

Emblem of the 21st Fighter Group, 455th Tactical Fighter Wing, Republic of China Air Force.

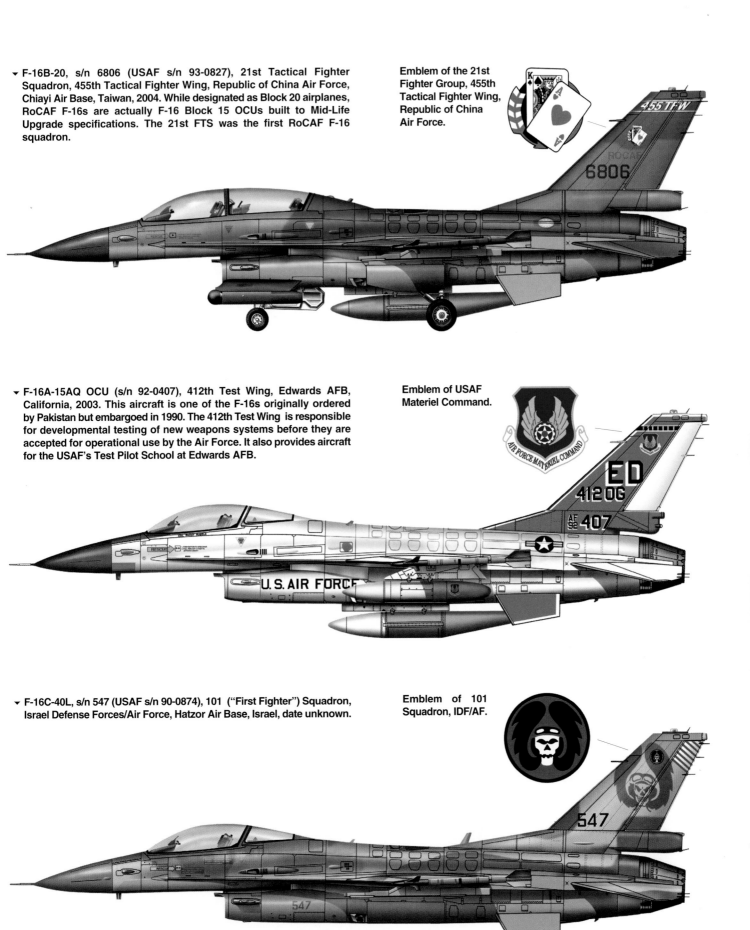

▾ **F-16A-15AQ OCU (s/n 92-0407), 412th Test Wing, Edwards AFB, California, 2003.** This aircraft is one of the F-16s originally ordered by Pakistan but embargoed in 1990. The 412th Test Wing is responsible for developmental testing of new weapons systems before they are accepted for operational use by the Air Force. It also provides aircraft for the USAF's Test Pilot School at Edwards AFB.

Emblem of USAF Materiel Command.

▾ **F-16C-40L, s/n 547 (USAF s/n 90-0874), 101 ("First Fighter") Squadron, Israel Defense Forces/Air Force, Hatzor Air Base, Israel, date unknown.**

Emblem of 101 Squadron, IDF/AF.

F-16C-40 (s/n 89-2001) 31st Fighter Wing, USAF, Aviano Air Base, Italy, 1993, during Operation Deny Flight, the United Nations enforcement of the "no-fly" zone over Bosnia-Herzegovina.

F-16C-42 (s/n 89-2098), 112th Fighter Squadron, 180th Tactical Fighter Wing, Ohio Air National Guard, Toledo, Ohio.

F-16A-15K (s/n 82-0938), 148th Fighter Squadron, 162nd Fighter Wing, Arizona Air National Guard, Tucson International Airport, Tucson, Arizona, 1997. As of September 2006, this aircraft was in storage at the Aerospace Maintenance and Regeneration Center, Davis-Monthan AFB, Tucson, Arizona.

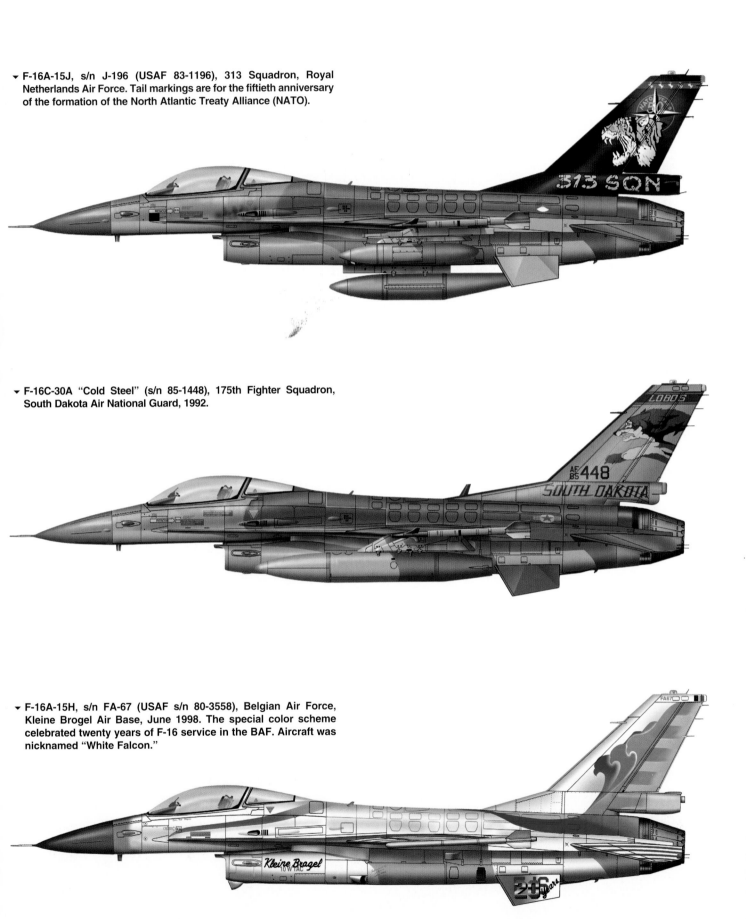

▾ F-16A-15J, s/n J-196 (USAF 83-1196), 313 Squadron, Royal Netherlands Air Force. Tail markings are for the fiftieth anniversary of the formation of the North Atlantic Treaty Alliance (NATO).

▾ F-16C-30A "Cold Steel" (s/n 85-1448), 175th Fighter Squadron, South Dakota Air National Guard, 1992.

▾ F-16A-15H, s/n FA-67 (USAF s/n 80-3558), Belgian Air Force, Kleine Brogel Air Base, June 1998. The special color scheme celebrated twenty years of F-16 service in the BAF. Aircraft was nicknamed "White Falcon."

▲ F-16C-50 (s/n 851) of Grupo 3, Fuerza Aerea de Chile (Chilean Air Force - FACh). In February 2002, Chile signed an agreement with the U.S. government to purchase ten F-16s in the Peace Puma Foreign Military Sales program, becoming the twenty-second customer for the F-16 worldwide and the second in South America. Derived from the Block 50+ configuration intended for Greece, Chilean aircraft (six C's and four D's) have AN/APG-68V(9) radar, an advanced electronic warfare package, and are able to carry conformal fuel tanks. The two-seat D-models are fully combat-capable and feature the same "large spine" fitted to Israeli and Singapore F-16Ds. They are equipped with the Joint Helmet-Mounted Cueing System and have Rafael Lightning II targeting pods. (Lockheed Martin)

South American F-16s

Chile

Venezuela

▲ Close-up of tail markings on a Venezuelan F-16A-15V (s/n 0220), Exercise CRUZEX 2004, Natal-Augusto Severo, Brazil, 16 November 2004. (Chris Lofting)

▼ F-16A-15V s/n 0220 (USAF s/n 84-1357), Grupo 16, Fuerza Aéra Venezolana (Venezuelan Air Force – FAV) lands at Exercise CRUZEX 2004. Tail markings celebrate twenty years of F-16 operations by Grupo 16. (Chris Lofting)

▲ F-16A-15K s/n 1041 (USAF s/n 82-1050) of the FAV's Grupo 16 taxies at CRUZEX 2004. (Chris Lofting)

▲ F-16A-15U s/n 0094 (USAF s/n 84-1349), Grupo 16, FAV, in standard camouflage. Of the FAV's original twenty-four F-16s, two have crashed due to engine failure, and the third, an F-16B, crashed during a maneuver during an air show at Aerea El Libertador Air Base, where Grupo 16 is based. The first and second commanders of the squadron were killed in the crash. The FAV sought U.S. government approval to replace these aircraft and was planning to overhaul and update the remaining airframes. In October 1997, the U.S. government approved the sale of two F-16s, as well as an upgrade packet including the F-100-PW-220E, but because of political considerations, the purchase of the attrition airframes has been halted until further notice. (Chris Lofting)

▶ A pair of ex-Dutch Vipers of the Fuerza Aerea de Chile (Chilean Air Force – FACh). In October 2005 the Chilean government decided to purchase eighteen Dutch F-16s (eleven A's and seven B's). The aircraft are already upgraded with the MLU conversion package and will be delivered between August 2006 and September 2007. This purchase will enable the FACh to create another F-16 squadron. (Lockheed Martin)

F-16
...still prowling the skies.

31 Tiger

FA-71

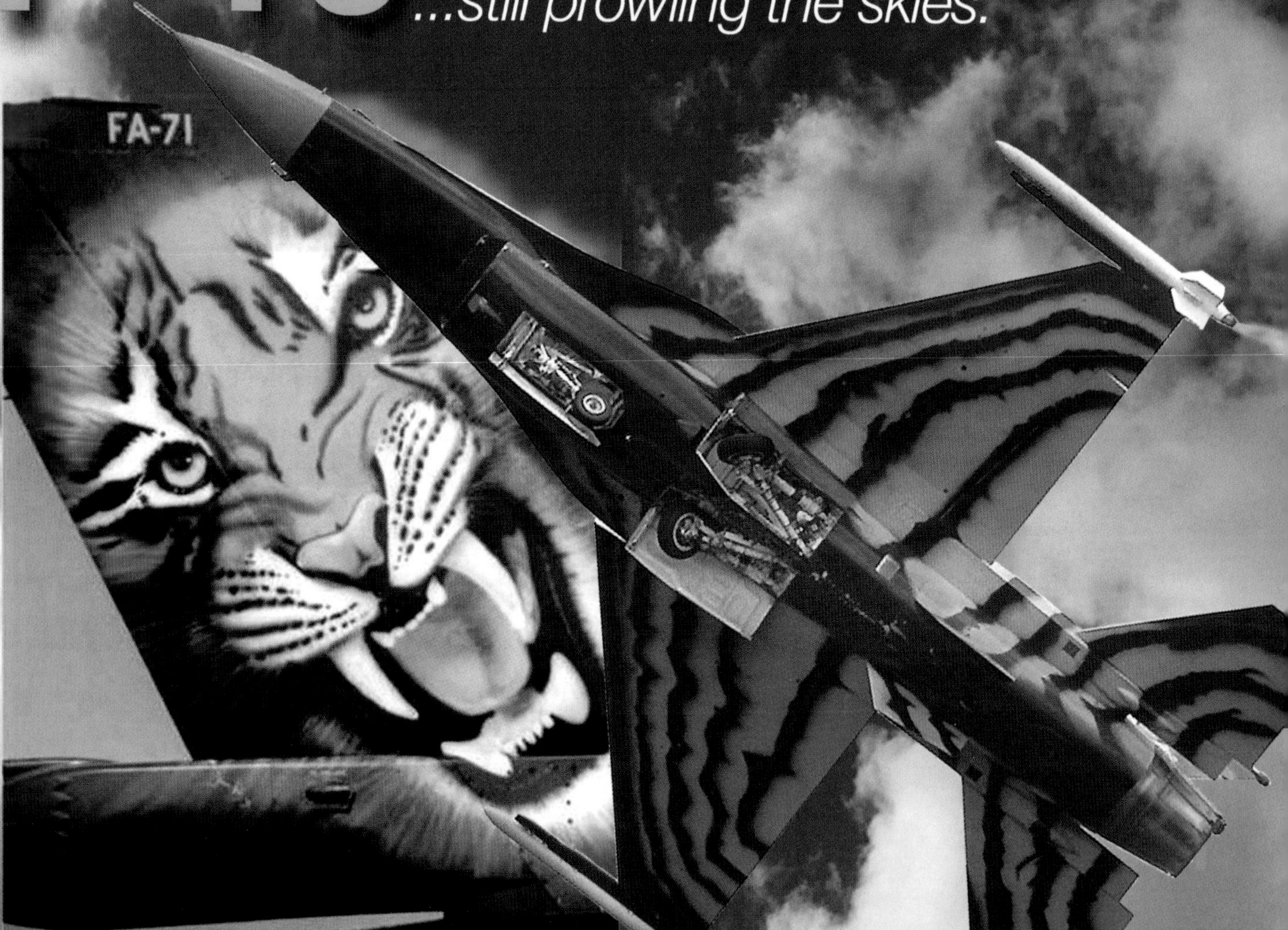

One of the world's most colorful Fighting Falcons was FA-71 of 31 Squadron, Belgian Air Force, painted in this spectacular scheme in 1998 to commemorate twenty years of F-16 service in the BAF. The markings also were used for the 1998 Tiger Meet and won the Silver Tiger Trophy. In spite of post-Cold War reductions in the BAF's F-16 fleet, FA-71 was operational as late as January 2006 ... still prowling the skies. (Stefaan Ellebaut and Cor van Gent)